Kol Isha:
Voice of the Woman
Poems in the Voices of
Women from the Bible

Susan H. Dubin

ISBN: **1540687007**
ISBN-13: **978-1540687005**

Table of Contents

Introduction
Voices of the Women: *Kol Isha*
Shekhinah, the female aspect of God

In the Beginning
Lillith, the first woman
Eve
Idit, Lot's Wife
Hagar's Plea
Devorah, Rebecca's Nurse

The Matriarchs
Sarai, Also Known as Sarah
Rebecca
Leah
Rachel

Women of Jacob, also known as Israel
Basemath, Esau's Wife
Bilhah's Lament
Dinah

Women of Joseph and His Brothers
Zuleika, Potiphar's Wife
Asenath, Joseph's Wife
Tamar and Judah

Women of the Exodus
Yocheved
Bat-Ya, Pharaoh's Daughter
Miriam's Song
Zipporah
***Kol Isha:* The Women at Sinai**

Women of the Wandering
Zelophehad's Daughters
Deborah's Song
Orpah
Ruth
Naomi

The Women of David and Solomon
Michal
Abigail
Maacah
Bathsheba
Tamar
Song of Shulammite

Women of the Two Kingdoms
Hannah
Delilah
Huldah
Jezebel
Judith

Women of Shushan
Vashti
Hadassah, Also Known as Esther

Kol Isha: **Voice of the Woman Shall Be Heard**

DEDICATION

For all the women in history who have not had their voices heard and for all the women yet to come. May the voice of the woman be heard throughout the land and bring its message of peace and equality.

ACKNOWLEDGMENTS

Many thanks to my many teachers and to the Rabbis who led the study groups that gave me the inspiration to write this book. Special thanks to my Los Angeles writing group – Rita Frischer, Dennis Cohen, Marcia Jacobs, Nancy Steiner, Terri Fox.

Introduction

Kol Isha means "voice of the woman." Although the Bible as a work of literature is replete with colorful characters who help define certain moral and ethical characteristics, most of the memorable main characters are male. In truth, many women people the pages of this story as well. In fact, women in the Bible are mentioned almost as often as their male counterparts. Many of these women, however, are merely mentioned by name, or alluded to in the text, but never fully fleshed out as characters.

In this work of poetry, I give a voice to major and minor female characters, some of whom are only mentioned in passing or not named at all, such as Idit, Lot's wife, or Zuleika, Potiphar's wife and Joseph's seducer. I also express through poetry the feelings and thoughts of some of the more well known women such as the Matriarchs. The poems are arranged roughly chronologically, grouping together women from the different periods of Biblical history.

In Biblical literature, poetry often uses the repetition of key words or phrases. I decided, therefore, that rather than rhyming verse, I would copy the biblical model in many of my poems. The poetic form varies from poem to poem to match the feelings of the character I am portraying. Although in most instances I assumed a general knowledge of the biblical story, I did retell some of the stories in order to give the emotions expressed some context. I have included a brief biographical note on all of the women along with information on where their stories can be found.

These poems express feelings of loneliness, alienation and disenfranchisement as well as wonder, hope, love, and joy. Although Biblical women lived thousands of years ago, I imagine that their feelings when confronted with the circumstances of their lives are universal. One reason the Bible has endured as a beloved piece of literature is that the characters peopling its pages confront life in ways that are relevant to people of today. Women need to have these Biblical models just as men do. It is time for the voices of women in the Bible, as well as the men, to be heard.

Voice of the Woman:
Kol Isha

Too long have I been silent.
My voice too long ignored.
Too long have I been silenced.
Now I must be heard.

Listen to my anger.
Recognize my pain.
Listen to my story.
It's time all know my name.

Shekhinah

"Let them make Me a Sanctuary so that my Shekhinah will dwell among them."
--Exodus 25:8

The Shekhinah is the female aspect of God. She is often portrayed as a gentle being who protects mankind by wrapping her cloak around those in need. Shekhinah derives from the Hebrew word *shekhan* which means "the act of dwelling." She is known as "the one who dwells among us."

In medieval times, the Shekhinah was seen as the Sabbath bride. The rabbis said the Shekhinah was present in every group of ten people who gathered to pray. In one story, she was described as the presence of God that appeared to Moses in the burning bush. Although Shekhinah is not mentioned as a name of God in the Torah, it is used in the Talmud and in later mystical writings of the Kabbalah.

Shekhinah

Hear me, daughters of the desert!
Listen to my voice, sons of the wilderness.
When your lives are harsh as the desert wind,
Call on me to bring you comfort.
In the depths of your despair,
Remember my love, and be consoled.

I am your Mother.
The edge of my gown will shelter you.
I am your Father.
Let me gather you in my arms and wrap you in the
protection of my robes.

Hear me, my children!
Be guided by my words of forgiveness.
Let loving kindness lead you to let go of your pain.
Dwell not in the wilderness of bitter memory.
Allow your names to be a blessing.
Listen to my voice, O, my children!

When time has erased all trace of your existence,
I will remember you, my sons of the wilderness.
When generations have long forgotten your sacrifices,
I will call your name, my daughters of the desert.

I am Shekhinah.
My love is without bounds.
I am Shekhinah.
My memory is eternal.
I am Shekhinah.

Listen and hear, O, my sons, O my daughters.

Susan H. Dubin

In the Beginning

Lilith

"He then created a woman for Adam, from the earth, as He had created Adam himself, and called her Lilith. Adam and Lilith began to fight. She said, 'I will not lie below,' and he said, 'I will not lie beneath you, but only on top. For you are fit only to be in the bottom position, while I am to be in the superior one.' Lilith responded, 'We are equal to each other inasmuch as we were both created from the earth.'"
<u>--Alphabet of Ben Sira</u>

Lilith is first mentioned in the 10th century mystical work entitled <u>The Alphabet of Ben Sira</u>. Scholars believe that the story of Lilith as told in this work comes from earlier Babylonian and Mesopotamian sources and that the name Lilith comes from the Akkadian spirit *Lilitu*. In the Bible story of creation, on the sixth day God created mankind, "male and female he created them." Later in the same chapter, the story of the creation of Eve from Adam's rib is recounted. Because of the two versions of the story, the rabbis felt a woman was created before Eve who was equal to Adam. Lilith is this first woman. The rabbis go on to say that when Adam tried to force her to lie beneath him during intercourse, she uttered the name of God and flew away to the Red Sea. There she mated with a fallen angel and produced one hundred demon offspring a day.

In Jewish folklore, she is portrayed as a she-demon who tries to kill newborn children. Newborns can be protected by amulets bearing the names of the three angels God sent to bring her back to Adam. She is also considered to be the mother of vampires and a symbol of sexual lust.

Lillith

I am known as
Baby stealer,
Heartbreaker,
Defiler.
Yet, it was Eve who disobeyed.

I did not eat from the Tree,
Nor did I tempt poor Adam.
But I am the one whose name is a curse.

Adam, other half of my soul, rejected me.
A partner was not to his liking.
He desired a helpmate.

Now, I must find my companions among the sons of
men.
But I will not love them.
My love was meant to be shared only with my twin soul.
It cannot be given to another.

If Adam had stayed with me,
We would have been equal partners in the Garden.
Now, let him get his bread by the sweat of his brow.
Paradise is lost to him.
It was lost when he rejected me.

Is my loneliness of so little consequence?
I, too, wanted a helpmate.
Why did You not take my rib?

Eve

"And Adam called his wife's name Eve; because she was the mother of all living."
--<u>Genesis 3:20</u>

In the biblical account, Eve was created from Adam's rib and was supposed to be a helpmate for him. God commanded Adam and Eve to care for the animals and plants found in the Garden of Eden, but warned them not to eat from the two trees in the middle of the Garden, the Tree of Knowledge of Good and Evil and the Tree of Life. Eve disobeyed God's command and ate from the Tree of Knowledge, thus causing mankind to be exiled from Eden.

Eve

All this beauty,
Eden,
Not enough.

My man,
Adam,
Not enough.

Eat the fruit
Or accept
DO NOT.

I have to know.
I want to decide.
I will not obey.

I would have eaten from that tree
Even if there were no snake.

Idit

"But his wife looked back from behind him, and she became a pillar of salt."
--Genesis 19:26

Although in the Biblical story she is not named, the Midrash (Rabbinic commentary on the Bible, Pirkei de-Rabbi Eliezer, Ch. 25) identifies Lot's wife as Idit. In the book of Genesis, God warns Lot and his family to leave Sodom, which is going to be destroyed by fire and brimstone because of the wickedness of its inhabitants. Lot and his family are told not to look back. Lot's wife disobeys and is turned into a pillar of salt. In trying to explain why she received such a harsh penalty, the rabbis say that Lot's wife gave away the presence of visitors to their home by asking a neighbor for salt. The evil inhabitants of Sodom then tried to harm these guests. Lot protected them by offering his daughters to the crowd in their stead. Being turned into a pillar of salt was a punishment that the rabbis saw as poetic justice.

Idit, Lot's Wife

"Do not look back!"
I was commanded.

I smelt the sulphur and heard the screams.
I felt the heat and tasted the ashes.
My tears were salt in my mouth.

"Do not look back!"

I left my friends, my neighbors.
Their values were not ours,
But I watched their children,
And they watched mine.

"Do not look back!"

Behind me is a life I grew to love.
There was the rug my mother gave us on our wedding
day.
There was the pot I used to cook our first meal.
There was the room where my daughters were born.

"Do not look back!"

So many memories.
How will I find a new life in this wilderness?
Who is this God that commands and destroys?

"Do not look back!"

But I must.
How can I leave without a backward glance?
Just one look for all I've lost…

Hagar

"And Sarah saw the son of Hagar the Egyptian, whom she had borne unto Abraham, making sport. Wherefore she said unto Abraham: 'Cast out this bondwoman and her son; for the son of this bondwoman shall not be heir with my son, even with Isaac.'"
Genesis 21:9-10

Hagar was an Egyptian woman, sometimes identified as a princess, who became a handmaiden to Sarah, Abraham's wife. As was the custom, when Sarah could not have children, she sent Hagar into her husband to bear a child for her. Ishmael, who is considered to be the father of the Arab nations, was the result of that union. Sarah, whose name was originally Sarai, and Abraham, whose name was changed from Abram, eventually had their own child. When God told Sarah that she would have a child, she laughed, and so she named the baby Isaac, which means laughter. Sarah, who was ninety when she became a mother, was very protective of her son. She felt that Ishmael was a bad influence on Isaac and forced Abraham to banish Ishmael and Hagar. Hagar cried out for God to protect her son, exclaiming that she couldn't watch Ishmael die of thirst in the desert. God sent an angel to protect them and reassured Hagar that her son would be the father of a great nation.

Hagar's Plea

Where have I wronged you, sister-wife?
Is it not for you that I went to Abram's bed,
To bear a child upon your knees?
Why do you hate me, sister-wife?
Am I not, like you,
Far from my home between the Two Rivers?
I am a princess,
Yet I serve your household like a bondswoman.
How far I have fallen.

Your jealousy has caused you to forsake me.
I lay with Abram at your command,
(Although I did not find the task unpleasant.)
Yet now you revile me.
You, who were mother-priestess, sister-mistress.
Our moon times sang together, yet you banished me.

You condemned me for my small pleasure.
You spoke to Abram, and he bent to your will.
I, an Egyptian princess, am banished, my son and I.
His taunts were not meant to harm your precious Isaac.
He merely laughed, as did you.

Ishmael cries in the desert.
But his cry is not ignored.
Your God, Abram's God, My God, hears him.
God's angel protects my Ishmael.
In the desert, I turned aside
So as not to watch my son die.
Now, I will see him live
To bear the seed of a great nation.

But, even now, it is not too late.
Welcome me home, Sarai.
If not for my sake, Princess, then for the sake of our sons.
They should be brothers.
They should be friends.
We could show them the ways of love.
Welcome me home, sister.

Devorah

"And they sent away Rebekah their sister, and her nurse, and Abraham's servant, and his men."
<u>Genesis 24: 59</u>

Devorah was a nurse and handmaid to the matriarch Rebecca. Rebecca was the daughter of Abraham's nephew Bethuel who lived in Padan-Aram, Abraham's family's ancestral home. Abraham sent his servant to Padan Aram to find a wife for Isaac, since he did not want Isaac to marry one of the Canaanite women. Rebecca saw the servant and offered him water for himself and his camels. She agreed to go with him to marry her cousin Isaac, and, of course, her nursemaid came with her. Later, the Bible mentions that Devorah also became the nurse for Rachel, Rebecca's niece and the woman who marries Jacob, the younger son of Rebecca and Isaac. It is curious that Devorah, a mere nursemaid, is one of the few women in the Bible whose death and burial place is described. The Bible says *"And Devorah Rebekah's nurse died, and she was buried below Beth-el under the oak; and the name of it was called Allon-bacuth."* **<u>Genesis 35:8.</u>**

Devorah, Rebecca's Nurse

Ah, look at him, my daughter.
See the stranger at the well, Rebecca.
He is handsome, is he not?
So well dressed, so well-mannered.
He must be the servant of a fine gentleman,
Just the one to whom you must go.

Speak to him, my daughter.
Offer water, for him and for his camels.
Here is your chance to seize your future.
He will bring all that I have wished for you.
You must have only the best.

When your mother died with you so young,
I became your parent, your teacher.
You are my child more than your father's, your mother's.

We will go with this stranger, this Eliezer.
His master is your kinsman, your Uncle Abraham.
You will make his son, Isaac, a fine wife.
There, with your cousin Isaac, is our life to be made.

If your future is assured, so will mine be.
I will go with you and guide you,
As I have always done.
You will be mother to a great nation,
And I will be remembered as the one who nurtured you.

Susan H. Dubin

The Matriarchs

Sarai, Also Known as Sarah

"And Abram and Nahor took them wives: the name of Abram's wife was Sarai; and the name of Nahor's wife, Milcah, the daughter of Haran, the father of Milcah, and the father of Iscah. And Sarai was barren; she had no child."
Genesis 11:29-30

Sarai was the wife of Abraham. Her name was changed to Sarah when God promised her a son as part of his covenant with Abraham. Sarai means princess. Sarah or Sarai was known for her great beauty. In fact, she was so beautiful, that when Abraham took her to Egypt, he made her promise to pretend to be his sister for fear that Pharaoh would kill him to possess her. Pharaoh did take Sarai, but was cursed with a plague by God, so he gave her back along with much gold and other goods including a bondswoman named Hagar. Unfortunately, Sarai could not give Abraham a child, so she sent her handmaid Hagar to Abraham to bear a child in her stead. When she was ninety, God promised her a child. She laughed when she heard that she would conceive. She did, however, finally give birth to Isaac whose name means "laughter." When Abraham took their son Isaac to Mount Moriah at God's command to sacrifice him, no mention is made in the Bible as to Sarah's thoughts. Shortly after this incident, however, Sarah dies.

Sarai

Do not remember me for beauty,
Even though mighty Pharaoh could not resist my charms.
Do not remember me for hospitality,
Even though the angels of the Lord ate at my table.
Do not remember me for protectiveness,
Even though I sent Hagar and her son
Away from my child into the desert.
Remember me as the mother of blessings,
The matriarch of Israel.

I gave my heart to the one God.
On his command I left my family and native land.
Ur, my home, was so beautiful.
I did not want to leave.
There I was known as Sarai, princess-priestess.
Then, Abram claimed me.
I gladly followed him and his one God,
But I cried many nights in the desert.

When we went down to Egypt,
Abram was afraid that Pharaoh
Might kill him because of my beauty.
So, I pretended to be his sister
And did not give him away,
Even when Pharaoh wanted me for his own.

When barrenness seemed to be my reality,
I willingly gave our servant Hagar to Abram
So she could bear him a child.
How it hurt me to see her belly big
When all I had were my slim hips and dry womb.

Finally, God saw into my heart and gave me Isaac.
I would have done anything to keep
This child of my old age safe.
But Abraham took our son
To be sacrificed on the mountain.
I thought my heart would stop when he left.
After Moriah, laughter left me.

I am known as Sarah, the first matriarch.
Remember me as I bless your daughters.
May laughter never leave them
And beauty be all they see.

Rebecca

"So let it come to pass, that the damsel to whom I shall say: Let down thy pitcher, I pray thee, that I may drink; and she shall say: Drink, and I will give thy camels drink also; let the same be she that Thou hast appointed for Thy servant, even for Isaac; and thereby shall I know that Thou hast shown kindness unto my master.' And it came to pass, before he had done speaking, that, behold, Rebekah came out, who was born to Bethuel the son of Milcah, the wife of Nahor, Abraham's brother, with her pitcher upon her shoulder."

Genesis 24:14-15

Rebecca is the second of the four matriarchs: Sarah, Rebecca, Rachel, and Leah. She married her cousin Isaac (Abraham and Sarah's son) and was the only one of the four women who did not share her husband with another woman. She had twin sons, Jacob and Esau. She favored mild mannered Jacob, while her husband Isaac favored the older twin Esau. Isaac became blind in his later years, and Rebecca advised Jacob how to take advantage of his father's poor eyesight to trick him into giving him the blessing and the birthright reserved for the oldest son.

Rebecca

All the way across the desert I rode to meet you,
My husband.
I left my home and my family, bringing only my maid,
Devorah.
I was so afraid.

But then I saw you coming towards us,
So tall, so handsome.
I could not wait and greet you like a proper maiden.
I leapt from my camel and ran into your arms.

After all these years together,
My heart still quickens when I see you,
Though your beautiful eyes see me no more.

I still believe you knew whose hands you touched.
The voice of Jacob could not be disguised
With rough pelts.
You surely knew your son when you blessed him.

I could not let you give the birthright to Esau.
He did not understand the ways of our God.
I have always been faithful,
Even when I was deceiving you.

Isaac, my love, have you forgiven me?

Leah

"Now Laban had two daughters: the name of the elder was Leah, and the name of the younger was Rachel. And Leah's eyes were weak; but Rachel was of beautiful form and fair to look upon."
<u>Genesis 29:16-17</u>

Leah was the oldest daughter of Laban, Rebecca's brother. Her sister Rachel was the first person Jacob, Rebecca and Isaac's son, met when he came to his uncle's house. He fell in love with Rachel and agreed to work for Laban for seven years as the bride price for marrying her. Laban, however, tricked Jacob and gave him Leah as his wife instead. Jacob then worked for seven more years to marry Rachel. Rachel had trouble conceiving, but Leah produced six sons and one daughter for her husband. Some Midrashic tales claim Rachel actually helped deceive Jacob into marrying Leah first because of her love for her older sister. In one rabbinic tale, Rachel and Leah are described as twins also, thus making the deception of Jacob a counterpoint to the deception of his father Isaac.

Leah

My eyes are not the eyes of beauty.
I see in shadows.
My eyes, my eyes are weak.

But my womb, my womb is strong.
I have born many sons.
They are strong men.
Men who love the sun.
Shepherds and herdsmen. Hunters.
They leave to guard the flocks.
They leave to make their own sons.

Yet, their father does not see them.
His eyes are only for Joseph,
Son of my sister of the beautiful eyes.
Her eyes, her eyes are strong,
But her womb, her womb is weak.

Does Jacob not know the need of strong sons for a
father's love?
Is Israel blind like his father Isaac?

My eyes, my eyes are weak,
But I, I can see.

Rachel

"And when Rachel saw that she bore Jacob no children, Rachel
envied her sister, and she said unto Jacob: 'Give me children or I
shall die.'"
Genesis 30:1

Rachel was the younger daughter of Laban and the wife of
Jacob and mother of Joseph and Benjamin. The Rabbis said that
Rachel and Leah were twins like Jacob and Esau and were in fact
supposed to marry the two brothers. When Esau turned away from
his mother's family and took wives from among the Canaanite
women, Jacob was given the task of marrying both sisters, the
Rabbis claim. Rachel, being the youngest, had to wait until Jacob
worked for her father for fourteen years before marrying him. Like
her aunt Rebecca and Jacob's grandmother Sarah, Rachel was
barren at first. She died in childbirth with her second son Benjamin
while journeying to Ephrath with her husband Jacob at God's
command. She was buried along the road that the Israelites later
followed when they were exiled from Jerusalem during the
Babylonian conquest.

Rachel

Waiting.
I am good at waiting.
I waited fourteen years for Jacob, my love.
I waited many more for my sons.
I am good at waiting.

When my father came to find his idols,
I waited in my red tent.
He never knew that I had taken them.
When Jacob took his turn
With Leah and Bilhah and Zilpah,
I waited.
After all, I was the one he truly loved.

I was good at waiting.
But Death did not wait for me.
He did not wait so I could see my children grow.
Maybe, if he had waited,
Joseph might not have earned the scorn of his brothers.
Benjamin might not have become a man
Without a mother.
The children of Israel might not have become
Slaves in Egypt,
Exiles in Babylon.

By the side of the road to Ramah I wait.
I weep for my children, the children of Israel.
I wait for my tears to soften the heart of God
And bring my children home.
I wait for the fulfillment of God's promise
To make my children a mighty nation.
How long must I wait?

Susan H. Dubin

Women of Israel

Basemath, Esau's Wife

"When Esau was forty years old, he married Judith the daughter of Beeri the Hittite, and Basemath the daughter of Elon the Hittite."
<u>Genesis 26:34</u>

Basemath is mentioned in the Bible twice. In the first passage, she is identified as the daughter of Elon, a Cannanite chieftain. She is also mentioned later in the story as a daughter of Ishmael. In both passages she is identified as Esau's wife, the mother of Reuel. Esau is considered to be the father of the Edomites, a Canaanite people who later fought with the Israelites.
.

Basemath, Esau's Wife

I was known in my land,
A desert princess.
Then, he came.
So strong, so handsome, with his hunter's arms
Covered with dark red curls.
How could I refuse him?
I became his wife, gave him strong sons.
But there was a sadness in his heart, a deep hurt,
A brother's betrayal.

I knew that he must heal that hurt.
Confront the brother who wronged him.
Learn to forgive.

Yet when they met,
I could only stand and watch
As this brother's household approached.
First the servants and herds and flocks,
Then the children and their mothers.
Behind them all, this brother
Who had stolen the birthright,
A smooth, gentle man.
And my husband, rushing toward him.
Esau, rushing forward with outstretched arms,
Greeting his brother with a kiss.

How different would our history be
If not for the gentle shove of a wife's concern.
My name should be known.

Bilhah

"And she said: 'Behold my maid Bilhah, go in unto her; that she may bear upon my knees, and I also may be builded up through her.' And she gave him Bilhah her handmaid to wife; and Jacob went in unto her. And Bilhah conceived, and bore Jacob a son."
Genesis 30:3-5

When Rachel finally married Jacob, her father Laban gave her Bilhah as a handmaid. After finding herself infertile, Rachel bade Bilhah to bear children for Jacob in her stead. Bilhah bore Jacob two sons, Dan and Naftali. Bilhah, who was purported to be very beautiful, also had a brief love affair with Jacob's older son Reuben, causing Reuben to be disinherited.

Bilhah's Lament

Although I am the mother of your mother's mother
Back many generations,
I am not one of the four mothers.
Still, I am the mother of your forefathers.

While Leah gave Jacob many sons,
Rachel was barren.
And so she sent me to bear a child upon her knees.

Ahh, Jacob was kind and virile
And I, too, loved him.
But my place was as a servant, a handmaiden.
Besides, his heart belonged only to Rachel.
How I envied her that love.
I suppose it was only fair
That she should envy me my children.

My sons will grow strong
And bring honor to this house.
Dan and Naphtali, good sons,
Two of the twelve of Israel.

I could never be honored wife.
I settled for Mother.

Dinah

"And Dinah the daughter of Leah, whom she had borne unto Jacob, went out to see the daughters of the land. And Shechem the son of Hamor the Hivite, the prince of the land, saw her; and he took her, and lay with her, and humbled her. And his soul did cleave unto Dinah the daughter of Jacob, and he loved the damsel…"
<u>Genesis 34:1-3</u>

Dinah, whose name is from the Hebrew root word meaning "judgment," was the only daughter of Jacob. Although Shechem first courted her by raping her, he later decided that he wanted to marry her. Jacob refused to speak to him or his father, but Jacob's sons agreed to let their sister marry Shechem and to let other Israelites marry the inhabitants of the kingdom if all the men agreed to be circumcised. When Shechem's countrymen were disabled after their mass circumcision, Dinah's brothers Simeon and Levi sought vengeance for her rape by slaughtering Shechem and his entire family and all the men of the city where they lived.

Dinah

I am the daughter of Israel.
I am the child of Jacob.
My name is Dinah, the one who has been judged.

My mother gave Jacob six sons and one daughter.
Yet, she was not Israel's favorite.
My father gave his love to Joseph
Of the many-colored coat.
Even before Shechem,
My tribe was not counted in the twelve.

That day I knew I should not wander in the fields.
I was an innocent maiden.
My dress was modest.
I cried out when he approached me.
I did not invite his touch.
I did not play the harlot.
Why should he think I asked to be taken?

But, after all, he loved me, did he not?
He wanted me to be his bride.
The bride price was cruel indeed,
The foreskins of all his kinsmen.
Still, he agreed, did he not?

That should have been the end of it.
Their discomfort for my innocence.
But that was not enough blood for my brothers.
So now I am widow before I am wife.

My name is Dinah, daughter of Jacob.
Why have I been judged not worthy to be counted as a
child of Israel?

Susan H. Dubin

Women of Joseph and His Brothers

Zuleika, Potiphar's wife

"And it came to pass after these things, that his master's wife cast her eyes upon Joseph; and she said: 'Lie with me.'
Genesis 39:7

Potiphar's wife is not named anywhere in the Bible. In Ginsberg's <u>Legends of the Jews,</u> however, she is referred to as Zuleika, which means "brilliant beauty" in Persian. A medieval Persian poet, Hakim Jami, wrote the story of a beautiful woman named Zueleika who dreamt of Yossuf or Joseph and became an actress who acted out the story of Joseph and Potiphar's Egyptian wife, Zuleika. Zuleika is first mentioned by name in Midrash where she is said to be so enamored of Joseph's beauty that she couldn't eat or drink. Potiphar, according to Midrash, was also supposed to be enamored with Joseph. In order to keep him from performing lewd acts, God made Potiphar impotent. Joseph's steadfast refusal to commit adultery caused him to earn Zuleika's enmity, and she finally accused him of rape. Potiphar threw Joseph in prison where his reputation for interpreting dreams eventually came to the attention of Pharaoh.

Zuleika, Potiphar's Wife

Joseph,
Beautiful boy,
Come to my bed.

Potiphar cannot love me.
My husband is impotent against my desire for you,
Your beauty has enslaved me.

Joseph,
I am lonely.
I cannot resist your beautiful face, your graceful form.

Burdened with his work for Pharaoh,
Potiphar trusts you with all his possessions.
He will not suspect.

Joseph,
I am your mistress.
Yet my desire for you has shackled my soul.

You do find me desirable.
Your lips may protest,
But I see that your body yearns for mine.

Joseph,
Lie with me
And all will be well.

If you do not obey me,
I will proclaim against you.
Who will take the word of a slave over the wife of
Pharaoh's favorite?

Asenath, Joseph's wife

"And Pharaoh called Joseph's name Zaphenath-paneah; and he gave him to wife Asenath the daughter of Poti-phera priest of On."
Genesis 41:45

Asenath is identified in some Midrash as the adopted daughter of Potiphar and Zuleika and in others as the daughter of Dinah (Joseph's half-sister) and Shechem. The first story can be explained because of the similarity in names of Potiphar and Poti-phera. According to The Jewish Encyclopedia, a Midrash says that Asenath was abandoned by Jacob under a thorn bush (senath in Hebrew) when she was an infant and found by Potiphar who took her home where he and his wife raised her as their own child. In another Midrash, Asenath is described as being a virgin who has never seen a man before Pharaoh gives her to Joseph. In the story, she immediately falls in love with Joseph because of his great beauty and accepts the Hebrew God of Joseph's family.

Asenath, Joseph's Wife

Tell me your dreams, my husband.
Now you are the beloved of Pharaoh,
But what of your own family, your kin?

I know naught of your life before you came to Egypt.
You have not shared that wound with me.
I have given you two strong sons,
Yet you do not trust me with your childhood.

I dream of eleven stars circling a brilliant sun.
I see a rainbow coat muddied with blood.
Explain these dreams, Joseph, my love,
You who interpret the dreams of Pharaoh,
Surely the dreams of your wife
Should be easy to explain.

Or, do you only know dreams of fat cows and thin,
Sheaves of wheat dancing in empty storehouses?

I pray that you sometimes dream of me, my love,
Dreams of longing and desire.
These are the dreams I dream of you.
Tell me your dreams, my love.

Tamar

"And it was told Tamar, saying: "Behold, thy father-in-law goeth up to Timnah to shear his sheep." So she put off from her the garments of her widowhood, and covered her head with her veil and wrapped herself, and sat down at the crossroads that were on the way to Timnah, for she saw that Shelah was grown up, and she was not given unto him to wife. When Judah saw her, he thought her to be a harlot, for she had covered her face. And he turned unto her by the way and said, "Come, I pray thee, let me come in unto thee," for he knew not that she was his daughter in law. And she said, "What will you give me that you should come to me?" And he said, "I will send thee a kid of the goats from the flock," and she said, "Wilt thou give me a pledge till thou send it?" And he said, "What pledge shall I give thee?" And she said, "Thy signet and thy cord, and the staff that is in your hand." And he gave them to her, and came in unto her, and she conceived by him."

Genesis 38:13-18

Tamar, a woman from Aram in Mesopotamia, was first married to Judah's oldest son Er who died on their wedding day before the marriage could be consummated. As was the custom, she then married Er's brother Onan. But, Onan did not want to have children with Tamar, because under the laws of that time they would bear the name of his brother, not him. Onan "spilled his seed upon the ground" rather than consummate the marriage and God slew him. Judah then promised Tamar to his youngest son Shelah, but neglected to arrange for the marriage when Shelah grew up. Under the laws of that time, Tamar could not take another husband and consequently could not have children, so she decided to solve her problem by seducing Shelah's father, Judah, after he became a widower by disguising herself as a ritual prostitute and waiting for him by the side of the road. When she became pregnant and confronted Judah, he admitted that he was wrong. Tamar bore twin boys, Perez and Zerah. Perez was the ancestor of King David.

Tamar and Judah

Ah, Judah, I hold your staff in my hand.
Your belt, too, I hold.
You cannot pretend that you owe me nothing.

When I came to your house as a young bride,
You gave me your first-born son,
But that match was not to be.
Your second son, too, came to my bed.
But he spilled his seed upon the ground and never lived
to love me.
I waited for your third son for many years.
I will not be left childless,
An empty shell of a woman, my purpose unfulfilled.

Your God's command to be fruitful and multiply was a
promise to me.
I have forced you to keep that promise.
When I played the harlot, you came to me.
Sometimes the father must fulfill the duties of his sons.
Sometimes a woman must remind a man of his duty and
his promise.

I bear your twin sons with no regrets.
They guarantee that your line will continue.
They have fulfilled God's promise to make Israel a
mighty nation.

Collect your pledges, Judah.
I have been paid.

Susan H. Dubin

Women of the Exodus

Yocheved

"And the name of Amram's wife was Jochebed (Yocheved), the daughter of Levi, who was born to Levi in Egypt; and she bore unto Amram Aaron and Moses, and Miriam their sister."
<u>Numbers 26:59</u>

Jochebed, or Yocheved in the Hebrew, is not named in the Biblical account of the birth of Moses in the Book of Exodus. She is finally identified in Numbers when the genealogy of the children of Israel is given. The Talmudists identify Yocheved with Shifrah, one of the midwives who defied Pharaoh's order to throw all male children born to the Israelites into the Nile. When her husband Amram divorced her rather than sire any babies who might be killed, her daughter Miriam convinced her parents to remarry stating that Pharaoh's decree only called for the death of male children, but if the Israelites had no children the whole nation would die. Yocheved then conceived and bore a son who would lead the Jewish people out of Egypt. She hid her infant son for three months before putting him in an ark made of bulrushes and setting him in the River Nile.

Yocheved

I am his mother.
A slave.
A Hebrew.
He has been hidden these weeks since his birth,
This child that almost didn't come to be.
And now
What am I to do?
I cannot hide him any longer.
His cries will condemn us all to death.
But I am his mother.
How can I set him afloat on the Nile?
This basket, so thin,
Protect my child.
Rock him to sleep.
Keep him safe.
Set him free.

Bat-Ya

"And the child grew, and she brought him unto Pharaoh's daughter, and he became her son. And she called his name Moses, and said: 'Because I drew him out of the water.'"
Exodus 2:10

Bat-Ya means the daughter of God. In <u>Legends of the Jews,</u> Ginsberg states that God "said to the princess: "Moses was not thy child, yet thou didst treat him as such. For this I will call thee My daughter, though thou art not My daughter," and therefore the princess, the daughter of Pharaoh, bears the name Batya, "the daughter of God."" When Moses led the Israelites out of Egypt, Batya went with them. She later married Caleb, one of the spies sent to check out the land of Israel.

Bat-Ya, Pharoah's Daughter

I know loneliness.
I, Bat-Ya, Daughter to a god who ruled the Two
Kingdoms,
I, Bat-Ya, daughter of Pharaoh, yet never to be queen.
I, Bat-Ya, sister to Pharaoh, but never to be wife.
I, Bat-Ya, loved by all,
But never beloved by my own belov'ed.

Once I was Mother to a child not my own,
But now he has gone to find his God.
He searches for peace within himself.
He yearns to set his people free.

Once I was at home among my people,
But now I am a stranger in my own land.
Where will I find peace?
Who will set me free?

I know loneliness.
I wander with the people of my son.
I search for freedom with their God.
I, Bat-Ya, daughter of the Nile,
I, Bat-Ya, daughter of God.
I, Bat-Ya, beloved of the One who rules the world.

Miriam

"And Miriam the prophetess, the sister of Aaron, took a timbrel in her hand; and all the women went out after her with timbrels and with dances."
Exodus 15:20

      Miriam, whose name means "bitterness," was the oldest child of Amram and Yocheved, the sister of Aaron and Moses. According to Midrash, she foresaw the birth of Moses and his role as a leader of the Jewish people. When her mother left the infant Moses in a basket on the Nile, Miriam watched him. She offered to find a wet-nurse for him when Pharaoh's daughter decided to adopt him, and she, of course, gave the job to her own mother. In Rabbinic commentary, Miriam is identified as Puah, the midwife who defied Pharaoh by refusing to kill Jewish babies. After the exodus, during the Israelites wandering in the desert, legend portrays Miriam as the keeper of a well of sweet water that followed her everywhere she went. When she died, the well disappeared. Her most well-known accomplishment, however, was as the leader of the women in song and dance at the Red Sea. For this she is called the Mother of Music.

Miriam's Song

I am Miriam.
Yocheved's only daughter.
Amram's outspoken child.
Aaron's jealous sister.
Moshe's watchful guardian.

I am Miriam.
Miriam of the Red Sea's song.
Miriam of the dance by the Sea of Reeds.
Miriam, the voice in the desert that will not be silenced.

I am Miriam.
Miriam of bitter loneliness.
Miriam of wild rejoicing.
Miriam, the keeper of sweet waters.

I am Miriam.
I dance for the tribe of Dinah.
I sing for the children of Israel.
I am Miriam.
Remember me.

Zipporah

"Then Zipporah took a flint, and cut off the foreskin of her son, and cast it at his feet; and she said: 'Surely a bridegroom of blood art thou to me.'"
Exodus 4:25

Zipporah was the daughter of Jethro and the wife of Moses. She is identified in the Bible as a Cushite or Ethiopian woman, not an Israelite. When on the way back to Egypt to talk to Pharaoh, God sought to kill Moses for failing to circumcise his son. Zipporah saved her husband by performing the circumcision, a rite which is incumbent upon a father to perform. She threw the bloody foreskin at Moses, and he left her behind when he went back to Egypt. Zipporah and her sons joined the Israelites after the Exodus on their march through the desert to the Promised Land.

Zipporah

I am Zipporah,
Desert princess,
Linked forever to my shepherd prophet,
Consort to God's chosen,
Stranger to his people,
Yet mother of blessings.

I wish to be like Sarah and Rachel.
Not the dark sister,
But a bringer of light.

I am not a singer like sister Miriam.
Nor can I dance.
But sacrifice I know,
And loneliness.

Not for me the timbrel and the lyre.
Not for me rejoicing on the shore.
I hold the bloodied knife
And remind my lord of his duty and his promise.

I am Zipporah,
Wife of Moses,
Daughter of Jethro,
Mother of Gershom, bridegroom of blood.

I am the stranger in your midst.
Welcome me as your God commands.

Susan H. Dubin

Women of the Wandering

The Women at Sinai

And Moses went up unto God, and the Lord called to him out of the mountain, saying: 'Thus shalt thou say to the house of Jacob, the sons of Israel...'
Exodus 19:3

According to the Hertz Commentary on the Biblical passages concerning the giving of the Torah, or law, at Mount Sinai: "Moses is bidden to approach the women first, as it is they who rear the children in the ways of Religion." According to Midrash, God asked each nation what they would give to guarantee that they were worthy to receive the Torah, and the women of Israel pledged their unborn children. God felt that the promise to teach their children the ways of the Torah was the highest pledge that could be given and the Torah was given to the Jewish people. However, later in the chapter, Moses warns the men to stay away from the women if they want to hear God's words, and the women were made to stand behind the men, not near Mount Sinai when God revealed his commandments.

Kol Isha: The Women at Sinai

Hear us, Elohim.
Speak to us, God of our mothers.
Our jewels bought our freedom in Egypt.
Our voices praised you at the Red Sea.
With our children we guarantee your Torah.

Look at us, Shadai.
We, too, are at the foot of the mountain.
We, too, see the lightning and hear the thunder.
We are here because we choose to accept your laws.

Speak to us now as we stand here at Sinai.
Give us the law as you have given it to our fathers and
brothers.
We, too, shall do all you have commanded.

In our tents we will worship you.
Our children will make your Sabbath holy.
No other gods will we put before you.
We will listen, and we will obey.

God of our Mothers,
Listen to the words of our hearts.
Grant us a voice.
Hear our prayers and answer us,
Adoneynu.

Zelophehad's Daughters

"Then drew near the daughters of Zelophehad, the son of Hepher, the son of Gilead, the son of Machir, the son of Manasseh, of the families of Manasseh the son of Joseph; and these are the names of his daughters: Mahlah, Noah, and Hoglah, and Milcah, and Tirzah."

Numbers 27:1

The five daughters of Zelophehad changed the laws of inheritance so that women could inherit property if a man died without a male heir. At the time of the Exodus, women were not counted in the census and had no legal standing. Zelophehad died in the wilderness without a son to inherit his portion of land when the tribes of Israel finally arrived in the Holy Land. The daughters confronted Moses and Eleazar the High Priest. Moses took their request to God who said, "The daughters of Zelophehad speak right; thou shalt surely give them a possession of an inheritance among their father's brethren; and thou shalt cause the inheritance of their father to pass unto them. And thou shalt speak unto the children of Israel saying: If a man die, and have no son, then ye shall cause his inheritance to pass unto his daughter."

Zelophehad's Daughters

Listen to the words of Mahlah, Noah, Hoglah, Milcah, and Tirzah.
Heed the voices of the daughters of Zelophehad.
We speak for the women who came before us.
We plead for the women who will come after.

Should we not be given our portion?
Like you, our fathers were AbrahamIsaacJacob.
The tribe of Joseph marks our lineage.
From Manasseh we are descended.

Heed the plea of the daughters of Zelophehad.
We worship the God who is God for male and female.
We, too, are bound by the laws of Sinai.

Listen to Mahlah, Noah, Hoglah, Milcah, and Tirzah.
Let the daughters of SarahRebeccaRachelLeah share in
the bounty of Israel.

Our souls should be counted
Among the children of Jacob.
We have as much right to be heard as any man.
Do not punish our father for having only daughters.
We will not hate you for having sons.

Listen to the Daughters of Zelophehad.
Heed Mahlah, Noah, Hoglah, Milcah, and Tirzah.
Give us our rightful portion in the land of milk and
honey.
Our plea is just. Count us.

Susan H. Dubin

In a New Land

Deborah

*Now Deborah, a prophetess, the wife of Lapidoth, she judged
Israel at that time. And she sat under the palm-tree of Devorah
between Ramah and Beth-El in the hill country of Ephraim; and
the children of Israel came up to her for judgment. And she sent
and called Barak the son of Abinoam out of Kedesh-naphtali, and
said unto him: 'Hath not the Lord, the God of Israel, commanded
saying: 'Go and draw toward Mount Tabor, and take with thee ten
thousand men of the children of Naphtali and the children of
Zebulon? And I will draw unto thee to the brook Kishon Sisera, the
captain of Jabin's army, with his chariots and his multitude; and I
will deliver him into thy hand.'"*
Judges 4: 4-7

Deborah is one of the better-known women in the Bible.
She was one of the Judges, or rulers of the Israelites in Canaan,
who is best known for her part in the battle against Sisera. The
verses known as the "Song of Deborah" are some of the oldest
known sections of the Bible. According to The Jewish
Encyclopedia, modern critics feel these lines were written very
near the time the battle described takes place and may have been
part of an early work called "Book of the Wars of YHWH."

Deborah's Song

Hear me, Sons of Israel!
Battle calls us.
We fight as God commands.
But our ways will not always be the ways of war.
Someday we will live in this land in peace.
Our hands will labor in the soil.
Our hearts will sing praises to the God of our fathers.

Hear me, Daughters of Miriam!
Prepare your timbrels and your lyres.
We sing to give our hearts courage.
We dance to lighten the heavy toll that war must bring.
But some day we will sing for children playing in the sun.
We will dance to music born of gladness.
Our souls will rejoice in the ways of the Lord of our
mothers.

Hear me, my people!
Today we tighten our belts and pick up the sword.
We follow Barak to his battle.
The hosts of Sisera shall be defeated.
By a woman's hand he shall die.
Tomorrow we will loosen our bonds and lay down our
weapons.
The inhabitants of this land will know peace.
Our people will be whole,
And all the world will praise the Lord, God.

Orpah

"And they took them wives of the women of Moab; the name of the one was Orpah, and the name of the other Ruth: and they dwelled there about ten years." **Ruth 1:4**

"And they lifted up their voice, and wept again: and Orpah kissed her mother in law; but Ruth cleaved unto her." **Ruth 1:14**

Orpah is mentioned in the <u>Book of Ruth</u> as one of the daughters-in-law of Naomi. When famine came to the land of Israel, Naomi and her husband and two sons moved to Moab. There they prospered, and the two sons married Moabite women, Ruth and Orpah. Unfortunately, Naomi's husband and her two sons died. Jewish law demanded that the widows marry a near kinsman and that the child of that marriage carry the name and inheritance of the first husband. Needless to say, finding a man willing to agree to marry a non-Jew under those circumstances would be difficult. Therefore, when Naomi decided to move back to Israel, she cautioned her daughters-in-law to stay in Moab. Ruth begged Naomi to let her come, and thus became a convert. Orpah heeded Naomi's advice and stayed behind. Legend says that Orpah later had four sons who were giants. Her son Goliath was slain by Ruth's descendant, David, and Orpah was killed by Abishai, one of King David's generals.

Orpah

I am alone now.

My husband is dead.
My father-in-law is also gone,
As is my husband's brother.
But still I had you, Mother Naomi,
And Ruth, my sister.
I know I am not the daughter of your flesh,
But you are the mother of my heart.
I did not share parents with you, Ruth,
But you are my chosen sibling.
And now you, too, must go.

So, I am truly alone.

I cannot come with you like my sister Ruth.
It is not because I love you less, Mother.
My home is not in Israel.
My people are not the children of Jacob.
My god is not the God of Abraham.
I would be a stranger in your land.

When you have returned to your home, Mother,
Will you remember me?

I knew happiness with your son.
He loved me,
And I loved him.
If he had lived,
I would still be your daughter.
My children would be part of your household.

But you have left me
In my own land.
I will never see your face again.
For this I weep.

Good-bye, Naomi.

Your Moabite daughter will sing your praises
Now and forever.

Good-bye, Ruth.

Hold the memory of your Moabite sister
In your heart.

Ruth

*"And Ruth said: 'Entreat me not to leave thee, and to
return from following after thee; for whither thou goest , I
will go; and where thou lodgest, I will lodge; thy people
shall be my people, and thy God, my God"*
<u>Ruth 1:16</u>

Unlike her sister-in-law Orpah, Ruth follows Naomi back to
the Land of Israel. Because the two women are so poor, Ruth
must glean barley from the fields of one of the rich men of
Naomi's village in order to have food for them to eat. The man
is Boaz, a descendant of Tamar and Judah, and a kinsman of
Naomi. Thanks to the advice of her mother-in-law, Ruth is able
to attract the notice of Boaz and eventually marries him.

Ruth

When I said that I would follow you,
I did not know where we would go.
I did not know who we would meet.
I did not know.

When I said that I would be one with your people,
I did not know how different our life would be.
I did not know how bitter you would become.
I did not know.

When I said that I would accept your God,
I did not know if your God would accept me.
I did not know if I could truly believe.
I did not know.

Now I know that when my husband died my life was not over.
Now I know that love can be mine again.
Now I know that happiness still awaits me.
Now I know.

Your people have shown me kindness and compassion.
Your kinsman has accepted my love.
Now I am a daughter of Israel even though I was born a stranger.
Now I am home.

Naomi

" 'Call me not Naomi, call me Marah; for the Almighty hath dealt bitterly with me. I went out full, and the Lord hath brought me back home empty.' "

<u>Ruth 1:20-22</u>

The story of Ruth took place, according to the Bible, during the time of the Judges. After both sons and her husband became ill and died, Naomi decided to return to her homeland. Her two daughters-in-law were upset about her decision to leave, but only Ruth decided to go with her mother-in-law. Naomi was very bitter about the loss of her husband and children, but cared for her daughter-in-law as if she were a blood relative. It was Naomi's sage advice that caused the marriage between Ruth and Boaz, Naomi's kinsman. Like many of today's grandmothers, Naomi became the nurse to their child, the grandfather of King David.

Naomi

How can I welcome this bride of my son?
She is not of my people.
She is not of my land.

And yet, she has been a faithful wife.
She has been a devoted daughter.

If she comes with me,
I will have to care for her.
I am afraid that my shriveled heart
Cannot make room for her devotion.

She claims that she desires only to make my people hers,
My home, her home,
My G-d, her G-d.
But what if she grows lonely for her own people,
Her own land, her own G-D?

I know not what awaits me in Bethlehem.
Maybe all she wants is my mother-love.
But I am a bitter woman
Who dares not promise anything.
If she leaves me, I will truly have nothing.
Can her daughter-love sweeten my sour soul?

Susan H. Dubin

The Women of David and Solomon

Michal

"And Michal the daughter of Saul came out to meet David and said, "How glorious was the king of Israel today, who uncovered himself today in the eyes of the handmaids of his servants, as one of the vain fellows shamelessly uncovereth himself!" And David said unto Michal, "It was before the LORD, who chose me before thy father and before all his house, to appoint me ruler over the people of the LORD, over Israel; therefore will I play before the LORD. And I will yet be more vile than thus, and will be base in mine own sight; and of the maidservants whom thou hast spoken of, of them shall I be held in honor." Therefore Michal the daughter of Saul had no child unto the day of her death."

Second Samuel 6:20-23

Michal was the younger daughter of King Saul. She is the only woman in the Bible who is quoted as saying she loved a man. Although King Saul promised to marry his oldest daughter Merav to the man who slew Goliath, he reneged when he learned that his rival, David, had accomplished the feat. He agreed to the marriage between Michal and David, because he thought that he could then find a way to trick David and murder him. David is first saved from Saul by Jonathan, Saul's son, who is also said to love David. Michal saves her husband from her father's men by lowering him out the window. Saul retaliates by taking Michal away and marrying her to another man. David later demands Michal's return, although the Bible does not record whether Michal wanted to be returned to a husband who had already endeared himself to the women of Israel. When David triumphantly brings the Ark of the Covenant to Jerusalem, Michal rebukes him for dancing naked in jubilation. She is cursed by David to die a barren woman.

Michal

I loved you once, David.
I begged my father to give me to you,
But Saul cared only for his kingdom
And for what price I could bring.

You wanted me.
You paid my father's price—one hundred Philistine
foreskins.
Or was it his crown you desired even then?

You left me to fight your wars and woo your women.
Were they enough for you?
Or did you hunger for my brother's love?
Is your soul still knit with Jonathan's,
A covenant between your house and his?

When you fled, my father gave me to the son of Laish.
I was happy there.
Palti, my husband wept when you took me in Bahurim.

Why did you take me back?
So I could watch you dance naked before the Lord?
Did you think I did not see all the women of Jerusalem
Cast their eyes upon you?
For them, you are the sweet singer of Israel.
To me, you are not husband, not king.
I know you as the bitter aftertaste of love.
You have left me a barren woman.

Abigail

"And when Abigail saw David, she made haste, and alighted from her ass, and fell before David on her face, and bowed down to the ground. And she fell at his feet, and said: 'Upon me, my lord, upon me be the iniquity…"
First Samuel 25: 23-24

Abigail was married to Nahor, a very wealthy man. When David and his soldiers camped in Nahor's vineyard, Nahor refused to give them hospitality. Abigail went to David and apologized for her husband. David was very impressed with Abigail's generosity and her great beauty, so when Nahor died a short time later, David asked Abigail to become his wife.

Abigail

My husband has wronged you.
You asked for food and comfort --
A boon you well deserve.
You have guarded our lands from those who waged war,
Protecting us from the Philistines.
All Israel says David has slain his ten thousand.

I did not see the men you sent to my home.
Upon me, my lord, be the sin of turning you away.
Have no regard for Nabal, my husband.

Let me wash your feet and feed you figs.
I, your handmaid, will offer you welcome.
Take these loaves and this wine.
Eat the lamb I have prepared for you.
Taste my sweet raisins.
Even now your praises are sung in Judea.

Forget the wrongs of my selfish husband.
When you are anointed king,
Remember your handmaid, Abigail.
I shall belong to you.

Maacah

*"His second [son], Chileab, of Abigail the widow of
Nabal of Carmel; the third, Absalom son of
Maacah, daughter of King Talmai of Geshur."*
Second Samuel 3:3

Maacah is listed as one of the wives of King David. She
was a princess in her own right, since she was the daughter of King
Talmai of the small kingdom of Geshur. "Geshur" in Hebrew
means "bridge", and the kingdom of Geshur was situated between
Judah and Israel, the two kingdoms that David united under his
reign. Maacah is also mentioned as the mother of Hanan,Tamar,
and Absalom. Hanan becomes a general in David's army. Tamar is
raped by her half-brother Amnon and goes to Absalom for refuge.
Against King David's wishes, Absalom kills Amnon in revenge for
his sister's defilement and he flees the country to live with his
grandfather, King Talmai. Absalom raises an army to rebel against
David, but he dies when he is caught by his long beautiful hair
during a battle in the revolt. Maacah's reactions to her children's
tragedies are not recorded, however, Absalom's daughter, the
mother of King Rehoboam, is named Maacah as well.

Maacah

Absalom, Absalom, my son.
Do not rise up against your father.
To be King is all he desires.

Absalom, my son, my son.
Do not hate him.
I was not his first wife or his second,
Yet once he wanted me.
David's heart, however, belongs only to his people and
his God.

Absalom, Absalom, my son.
When Tamar, your sister, was taken by your brother
Amnon,
You comforted her.
For her sake you slew your brother.
You have gone to my father's house,
And David cries out for you.

Absalom, my son, my son.
You stole the hearts of Israel.
In Hebron you gather the young men.
The people are in love with you.
You have entrapped them with your long hair and
beautiful face.

Absalom, Absalom, my son.
David has fled his house.
Do you truly seek his death?
Your father is a good king,
He loves you.
For my sake, Absalom, my son, my son,
Do not hate him.

Bathsheba

"It happened, late one afternoon, when David arose from his couch and was walking upon the roof of the king's house, that he saw from the roof a woman bathing; and the woman was very beautiful. And David sent and inquired about the woman. And one said, "Is not this Bathsheba, the daughter of Eliam, the wife of Uriah the Hittite?" So David sent messengers, and took her; and she came to him, and he lay with her .... And the woman conceived; and she sent and told David, "I am with child."
Second Samuel 11:2-5

The name "Bathsheba" literally means "daughter of the oath," but her name has become synonymous with adultery and lust. Described in the Bible as "beautiful," she is seen by King David as she is taking a bath. Although she is married to one of David's most trusted soldiers, Uriah the Hittite, David is smitten with her and commands that she lay with him. They conceive a child who dies after living for only seven days. Many biblical commentators claim that the death of the child was the price David had to pay for stealing another man's wife and sending that man to his death in battle. The Bible, however, never indicates that Bathsheba was taken against her will. In fact, David and Bathsheba are portrayed in later literature and art as one of the most romantic couples in Biblical writings. After the death of her husband, Bathsheba and David marry. To comfort his wife after the death of their infant son, David lays with her and they conceive another child, Solomon. Solomon becomes king after David and is known for his wisdom and his beautiful love poetry in the Song of Songs.

Bathsheba

Why did you choose me,
My shepherd, my love?
My duty was to my husband, not my king.
Yet, you commanded and I obeyed.

We have sinned,
My king, my love.
Our bodies called to each other from the rooftop,
And we were powerless to resist.

I was not unwilling,
My shepherd, my love.
I found you so desirable.
Your song awoke my heart,
Your sweet music sang to my soul.

We have sinned,
My king, my love.
But I would not have it any other way.
I have known the sweetness of my beloved's kiss,
I have tasted the nectar from his lips.

Perhaps our son will redeem our love.
In his wisdom he will know
That you are my beloved and I am yours.
One day, he will hear the call of the turtledove,
And answer with a song.

Tamar

"Now Absalom, David's son, had a beautiful sister, whose name was Tamar; and after a time Amnon, Davids son, loved her."
Second Samuel 13:1

"But he would not listen to her; and being stronger than she, he forced her, and lay with her. Then Amnon hated her with very great hatred; so that the hatred with which he hated her was greater than the love with which he had loved her. And Amnon said to her, "Arise, be gone."
Second Samuel 13: 14-15

Tamar was the daughter of King David and Queen Maacah and the sister of Absalom. Amnon was her half-brother. He desired her so much that he became ill and begged his father to send Tamar, who was a virgin, to him to bring him some food. King David commanded Tamar to visit her half brother. However, Amnon raped her and threw her into the street. Her brother Absalom took her in and counseled her to keep silent about the rape. She agreed, but according to the Bible "remained desolate." Absalom took revenge on Amnon two years later by ordering his death. This act caused a rift between David and Absalom that ended with Absalom in rebellion and his death at the hand of his father. Tamar is not mentioned again.

Tamar

Brother!
I trusted you.
What have you done, Amnon?
You deflowered me
And threw me out.

Brother!
You stole my innocence.
I am left with nothing, Amnon.
Now no one will want me.

Brother!
I loved you once.
I would have died for you, Amnon.
But you have left me as good as dead.

Brother!
I have nowhere to turn.
Who will welcome me now, Amnon?
Perhaps our brother Absalom will take me.
But what will he do to you?

Brother!
You did not care for me,
Except in your lust, Amnon.
Why do I care what happens to you?
I will go to Absalom.
But can I truly trust a brother?

Shulammite

"My beloved spoke, and said to me,
"Rise up, my love, my beautiful one, and come away.
For, behold, the winter is past.
The rain is over and gone.
The flowers appear on the earth.
The time of the singing has come,
and the voice of the turtledove is heard in our land.
The fig tree ripens her green figs.
The vines are in blossom.
They give forth their fragrance.
Arise, my love, my beautiful one,
and come away."
Song of Songs 2: 10-14

Shulammite is the feminine form of the Hebrew name for Solomon, *Shlomo*. Both come from the root word *shalom*, meaning peace or wholeness. The Song of Songs is attributed to King Solomon, although some biblical scholars feel that at least some parts of the poem were written at a much later time. Most biblical critics feel that the poem is a dialogue between two lovers, Shulammite and her shepherd boy, who could also be King Solomon. Others, including the Rabbis, consider the poem to be an allegorical reference to the love that God has for Israel. The graphic descriptions of the lovers, however, seem to point to very human interaction and a universal expression of the passion that is felt by those in love.

Song of Shulammite

Come, come to me, my love, my fair one.
I am the one for whom your soul seeks.
Come to me.
Taste the honey of my lips.
Sip the spiced wine of my kiss.

I yearn for your love, my shepherd, my fair one.
My breasts are like two fawns,
Waiting in the field.
My navel is a round goblet,
Ready to overflow with your love.
Come, come to me.

Return, my love, my fair one.
I wait for you in the garden.
Surely you will come to me.
You have tasted my grapes and pomegranates.
Return, my beloved.

My vineyard, O Solomon, is yours.
Make haste, my beloved.
I wait by the bed of spices.
The fragrance of our love surrounds me.
Embrace me with your right hand.
Set me as a seal upon your heart.
Look into my eyes and know peace.

Susan H. Dubin

Women of the Two Kingdoms

Hannah

"Now Hannah, she spake in her heart; only her lips moved, but her voice was not heard: therefore Eli thought she had been drunken. And Eli said unto her, 'How long wilt thou be drunken? put away thy wine from thee.' And Hannah answered and said, 'No, my lord, I am a woman of a sorrowful spirit: I have drunk neither wine nor strong drink, but have poured out my soul before the LORD.'"
First Samuel 1:13-15

Like the matriarchs Sarah and Rachel, Hannah was barren. Her husband Elkanah had two wives, Hannah and Penninah. Penninah had children, and taunted Hannah with her barrenness. When Elkhanan traveled to make sacrifices at the Holy Temple, Hannah went with him. Eli, the High Priest, mistook her silent prayer for a drunken stupor. Hannah promised God that if she conceived a child, she would give him to the priests to raise in the service of the Lord. Her prayer was answered, and she became the mother of Samuel, the great prophet who anointed King Saul and King David.

Hannah

Drunk?
They dare to call me drunk.
Drunk?
They cannot see my breaking heart.
They do not hear my fervent prayer.

My lips move, but produce no sound.
They do not need to hear my words.
The cry of my soul is only for God's ears.

What can a man know of a barren woman's anguish?
How can even a High Priest understand
The empty space in my hollow soul?

Sarah would understand, and Rachel.
They knew the ache that only a child of one's own can
ease.

Ahh, I would give all I possess,
My sanity, my character, my good name,
If only God would give me a son.
Nothing, nothing, nothing can erase this pain
Except my own child.

I promise him to, you, God.
My child will belong to you.
Just let me hold him and hear his cry.

Drunk?
I am only drunk with grief and longing.
I am only drunk with hope.

Delilah

"That he told her all his heart, and said unto her, 'There hath not come a razor upon mine head; for I have been a Nazarite unto God from my mother's womb: if I be shaven, then my strength will go from me, and I shall become weak, and be like any other man.' And when Delilah saw that he had told her all his heart, she sent and called for the lords of the Philistines, saying, 'Come up this once, for he hath showed me all his heart.' Then the lords of the Philistines came up unto her, and brought money in their hand."
Judges 16: 17-18

Delilah was a Philistine woman beloved by Samson, the great Israelite warrior, who was said to have great strength. He fought many successful battles against the Philistines, who bribed Delilah to seduce Samson and find out the secret of his great strength. Delilah found out that Samson was a Nazarite, a religious sect that pledged themselves to God, swore to never cut their hair, or drink strong wine. After Delilah's betrayal, Samson's hair was cut, he lost his great strength and was captured by the Philistines who put out his eyes and put him to work in their prison. On a festival to their god, Dagon, they brought Samson out to their Temple to make fun of him. Samson prayed for one last burst of strength. He used it to pull down the pillars holding up the Temple, killing the Philistines who were there and himself. Although Delilah is not mentioned again in the text, it is reasonable to assume that she died with her countrymen at the Temple.

Delilah

As these walls crumble around me,
I yearn for the tenderness of your strong arms.
I wish you had let our love conquer our differences,
But now you and your God want only vengeance.

If you had renounced your God
And sworn your love for me,
I would have saved you, I think.
When I cut your hair,
You looked at me with such pain.
I almost regret what I have done.
No man could tame you,
But I seduced my way into your heart.
My people called on me to help.
Your God is not my god.
Perhaps I would have helped my people
Even if I had not been paid.
When you whispered to me the secret of your strength,
I rejoiced at the thought of sharing your weakness.

You boasted of your strength.
But, here, in the Temple court,
You were chained and blinded.

No!
Your rage pulled down the Temple walls.
Now we are powerless to change our fate.
Destruction and death is our only destiny.
Samson, I really did love you.
How could I not?
You were beautiful with your long, flowing curls.

Huldah

"So Hilkiah the priest, and Ahikam, and Achbor, and Shaphan, and Asaiah, went unto Huldah the prophetess, the wife of Shallum the son of Tikvah, the son of Harhas, keeper of the wardrobe (now she dwelt in Jerusalem in the second quarter); and they communed with her. And she said unto them, 'Thus saith Jehovah, the God of Israel: Tell ye the man that sent you unto me, Thus saith Jehovah, Behold, I will bring evil upon this place, and upon the inhabitants thereof, even all the words of the book which the king of Judah hath read.'"
Second Kings 22: 14-16

Huldah, whose name means "weasel," joins Miriam and Deborah as one of only three women identified as prophets in the Bible. Because she kept the untainted copies of the laws of Moses, she can be looked upon as a librarian of her day. Her husband Shullam (from the root word for "peace") was a royal tailor and the son of Tikvah (meaning "hope").

When King Josiah sought to repair the Temple, his workmen found a copy of one of the books (probably Deuteronomy), and Josiah sought to have it authenticated. The book proclaimed that there would be dire consequences for not following the law. Josiah probably asked for Huldah's opinion about the book, rather than her contemporary prophet, Jeremiah's, because Jeremiah's prophecies were always so harsh. Huldah sent word to the King that the words in the book were true: Israel would suffer, but Josiah himself would die a peaceful death.

Huldah

Listen to me, men of Judah!
I speak the word of God.
The scroll you bear is the Law.
Tell King Josiah that it must be obeyed.

The Prophet Jeremiah speaks of doom,
So you seek the gentler voice of a woman.
But I must guard the truth,
Even if speaking it displeases my king.

As a keeper of the scrolls,
I know God's words.
What is written will be.
Israel will be destroyed
Unless all hearken to God's commands.

Shullam, my husband, is a man of peace.
His father was a man of hope.
But there can be no peace,
There will be no hope,
While men sing praises to Balaam
And forget the Lord.

Tell your king,
Because he is a good man,
He will not see God's wrath.
I, Huldah, the prophetess give him my word.

Jezebel

"And it came to pass, when Jezebel heard that Naboth was stoned, and was dead, that Jezebel said to Ahab, 'Arise, take possession of the vineyard of Naboth the Jezreelite, which he refused to give thee for money: for Naboth is not alive, but dead.'
And it came to pass, when Ahab heard that Naboth was dead, that Ahab rose up to go down to the vineyard of Naboth the Jezreelite, to take possession of it. And the word of the LORD came to Elijah the Tishbite, saying, 'Arise, go down to meet Ahab king of Israel, which is in Samaria: behold, he is in the vineyard of Naboth, whither he is gone down to possess it. And thou shalt speak unto him, saying, Thus saith the LORD, Hast thou killed, and also taken possession? And thou shalt speak unto him, saying, Thus saith the LORD, In the place where dogs licked the blood of Naboth shall dogs lick thy blood, even thine.'"
First Kings 21: 15-19

Jezebel is arguably the most reviled of women in the Bible. She was considered a harlot and an evil woman. In the Biblical text, she was portrayed as a foreign princess who convinced her husband King Ahab to make the worship of Baal and Astarte the state religion of Samaria. Her daughter, Athaliah, was the only woman to rule Israel as Queen, and made the worship of the idols of Astarte and Baal the dominant religion of both the kingdoms of Samaria and Judea. Although she was, in reality, acting to preserve her own religion, Jezebel was hated by the prophets, especially Elijah, who was her contemporary. Jezebel was responsible for the murder of hundreds of priests of Israel, and arranged for the famous contest between Yahweh and Baal where the priests of Baal were struck by lightning and killed to prove Yahweh's power. Having been raised as royalty in her homeland of Phoenicia, she was used to getting whatever she demanded. When her husband Ahab desired the vineyard of Naboth, she arranged for Naboth's murder. This vicious, cold-blooded act caused Elijah to curse her, saying that she would die a horrible death and her blood would be the food of dogs. She was killed by being thrown out a window in the palace, and her blood was, indeed, lapped up by the dogs.

Jezebel

Ashteroth, Baal, Save me!
I sang to you.
I danced for you.
I sacrificed in the high places.
Your priests ate at my table,
But, now, you gods know me not.

I seduced Israel's king in your holy names.
As princess of Phoenicia, as priestess of Astarte,
I married King Ahab.
I brought his people to your holy groves.
My husband built your temple in Samaria,
Yet you do not answer my prayers.
If the priests of the Israelites have their way,
I will be food for dogs.

When Ahab desired the vineyard of Naboth,
I procured it for him.
I am a queen who fulfills desires.
Condemn me not to death
As you did those
Who sacrificed in your name on Mount Carmel.
Yahweh is a jealous God.
He wants vengeance for my joyous sins.
Show His prophet my gods will protect me.

Save me, Ashteroth, Baal, in the name of God!
I am Jezebel, Daughter of King Ethbaal.
I rule as I see fit.
I do not answer to Yah-weh's laws.
I worship whom I please. I am Queen.

Judith

"She went up to the post at the end of the bed, above Holofernes' head, and took down his sword that hung there. She came close to his bed and took hold of the hair of his head, and said, "Give me strength this day, O Lord God of Israel!" And she struck his neck twice with all her might, and severed it from his body."
Judith 13: 6-8

      The <u>Book of Judith</u> is not part of the Hebrew Bible. It, like the <u>Book of Maccabees</u>, is part of the Apocrypha. The <u>Jewish Encyclopedia</u> says that it was a story written for "household reading," akin to a modern day historical novel. The story takes place during the reign of Nebuchednezzar, after the Jews have returned to Palestine. The Jewish people are under attack by the Assyrians who are lead by an almost invincible general, Holofernes. Holofernes lays siege to the town of Bethulia, which stands in his way on his march towards Jerusalem. In the story, the people of Bethulia despair and are ready to surrender, but the town is saved when a righteous woman living there, Judith, ingratiates herself with Holofernes and manages to kill him.

      The name *Judith* translates as *Hebrew woman*, the author's attempt to make the heroine a symbol of hope for the Jewish people in times of trouble. Scholars feel the story was probably written around 100 B.C.E. in Hebrew. The earliest versions are Greek translations of the original, and the book was first quoted by Clement of Rome in the first century of the Common Era.

Judith

Listen, people of Bethuliyah!
Slack your thirst.
Satisfy your hunger.
You have nothing more to fear.
The siege of the Assyrians is ended.
Rejoice in their defeat
At the hands of a mere woman.

When you were ready to surrender,
I entered their camp.
You scoffed at my plan to bring us victory.
You asked, "What can a mere woman do?"
I offered their general my salty cheese and heady wine.
He gladly ate and drank his fill.
While he slept in his drunkenness,
I swung his sword and sliced off his head.
It was not bravery but duty that gave me strength.

You were ready to surrender,
But I, a poor widow, have brought you the head of the
one you feared.
Stick it on your gates to prove how the mighty
Holofernes
Fell to a mere woman.

Susan H. Dubin

Women of Shushan

Vashti

"On the seventh day, when the heart of the king was merry with wine, he commanded Mehuman, Biztha, Harbona, Bigtha, and Abagtha, Zethar, and Carcas, the seven chamberlains that ministered in the presence of Ahasuerus the king, to bring Vashti the queen before the king with the crown royal, to show the people and the princes her beauty: for she was fair to look on. But the queen Vashti refused to come at the king's commandment by his chamberlains: therefore was the king very wroth, and his anger burned in him."
Esther 1: 10-12

Queen Vashti was the first wife of King Ahasuerus of Persia. Her name, according to the Jewish Encyclopedia, was that of an Elammite Goddess, and she was supposed to be the great, great granddaughter of Nebuchadnezzar. According to Ginsberg in Legends of the Jews, Vashti refused to appear not because of any feminist leanings, but because the angel Gabriel had put a tail on her or turned her into a hermaphrodite. The rabbis in Midrash say she refused out of vanity, because she had sores on her face, possibly leprosy. Whatever the true reason, Vashti has become a symbol of Jewish feminism in her refusal to acquiesce to the king's command.

Vashti

He banished me.
I would not dance
So he banished me.

Every night he called me to him.
I did not refuse.
My duty as queen was to serve my king.

"Wear only your crown," he commanded.
He wanted my beauty to dazzle those drunken men.
Dance naked before his guests?
Hardly a fit request of a queen.

My charms are for him alone.
So, I refused.
I dance for no man against my will!

Let him find another queen to do his bidding.

Hadassah

"And he brought up Hadassah, that is, Esther, his uncle's daughter: for she had neither father nor mother, and the maiden was fair and beautiful; and when her father and mother were dead, Mordecai took her for his own daughter. So it came to pass, when the king's commandment and his decree was heard, and when many maidens were gathered together unto Shushan the palace, to the custody of Hegai, that Esther was taken into the king's house, to the custody of Hegai, keeper of the women. And the maiden pleased him, and she obtained kindness of him; and he speedily gave her her things for purification, with her portions, and the seven maidens who were meet to be given her out of the king's house: and he removed her and her maidens to the best place of the house of the women. Esther had not made known her people nor her kindred; for Mordecai had charged her that she should not make it known."
Esther 2: 7-10

The story of Esther is told in one of the five Megillot (scrolls) that make up the portion of the Bible called Ketuvim (Writings). She is identified as an orphan named Hadassah who is brought up by her cousin Mordecai. She is chosen in a beauty contest to be the second wife of King Ahasuerus of Persia. She is credited with saving the Jewish people of Shushan from destruction by foiling the plot of the king's evil advisor Haman. Her name *Hadassah* in Hebrew means *myrtle*. *Esther* is a Persian name, meaning *star,* and comes from the name of the goddess Astarte.

Hadassah, Known as Esther

I could not even keep my name.
Hadassah, sweet myrtle.
I could not keep my name.
No one must know that I am a Jew.

I became Esther.
The morning star.
A Persian maid.

My Lord chose me.
The king chose me.
I was chosen to be Queen.

Now I am locked in the palace.
I miss my people.
I miss my home.

Cousin Mordecai still comes.
He listens to my lonely tears.
He tells me to be strong.

He promises I will make the right choice.
He will guide me when the time comes.

But, how?
I am only a sweet myrtle, not a star.

Kol Isha: Voice of the Woman

At last,
The woman's voice shall be heard in the land.
We sing our past,
We celebrate our future.
Our lives are intertwined with yours.

Hear the voices of the women!
We open our mouths with wisdom.
Strength and dignity are our clothing.
Let our works praise us
And call our names a blessing.

Listen to our anger.
Recognize our pain.
Listen to our stories.
It's time all know our names.

ABOUT THE AUTHOR

Susan Dubin is the library consultant to the Sperling Kronberg Mack Holocaust Resource Center located in Las Vegas. This position led her to work with the World Federation of Jewish Child Holocaust Survivors and Descendants, Generations of the Shoah International, and Association of Holocaust Organizations in organizing their international conferences. As a library consultant, she provides classes for Clark County School District teachers and students. In addition, she organizes community events that feature authors, artists, and musicians. As a career teacher and librarian, Susan served as international president of the Association of Jewish Libraries. She was also on the board of the Southern California Children's Literature Council and California School Library Association. She has participated as a judge in many literary awards committees, and helped to organize the Once Upon a World Award from the Simon Wiesenthal Center Museum of Tolerance.

If Susan is not working or travelling, she is most likely reading. As an award-winning librarian, Susan can't resist a good book!

Made in the USA
Columbia, SC
11 May 2019